OCEAN LIFE
DICTIONARY

An A to Z of ocean life

Author Clint Twist
Editor Elise See Tai
Art Director Miranda Kennedy
Art Editor Julia Harris
Production Director Clive Sparling
Consultant Zoologist Valerie Davies
Illustrators Richard Bonson (The Art Agency), Robin Bouttell (The Art Agency), Barry Croucher (The Art Agency), Nick Hardcastle (The Art Agency), Myke Taylor (The Art Agency). Andromeda Children's Books would like to apologize in advance for any unintentional omissions.

Created by Pinwheel
A Division of Alligator Books Ltd
Winchester House, 259–269 Old Marylebone Road,
London NW1 5XJ, UK
www.pinwheel.co.uk

This edition produced in 2007 for Scholastic Inc.
Published by Tangerine Press, an imprint of Scholastic Inc.
557 Broadway, New York, NY 10012

Scholastic and Tangerine Press and associated logos are trademarks of Scholastic Inc.

ISBN-10: 0-439-93093-6
ISBN-13: 978-0-439-93093-2

Printed in Malaysia

Information icons

Throughout this dictionary, there are special icons next to each entry. These give you more information about each creature.

Size comparison pictures

Next to each entry you will see a symbol, either a hand, an adult human, or a diver next to a red icon of the creature listed. The symbol shows you the size of each creature in real life compared to the size of a human.

7 inches

The first symbol is a human adult's hand, which measures about 7 inches (18 cm) from the wrist to the tip of the longest finger. Some creatures are smaller than this, so this symbol helps you to imagine their size.

6 feet

The second symbol is an adult human. With arms outstretched, the arm span measures about 6 feet (1.8 m). The height of the human is about 6 feet (1.8 m). This symbol helps you to compare the height or length of a creature to a human.

6 feet

The third symbol is an adult diver. The length of the diver measures about 6 feet (1.8 m) from head to toe. This symbol will help you to imagine the length of some creatures.

OCEAN LIFE
DICTIONARY

An A to Z of ocean life

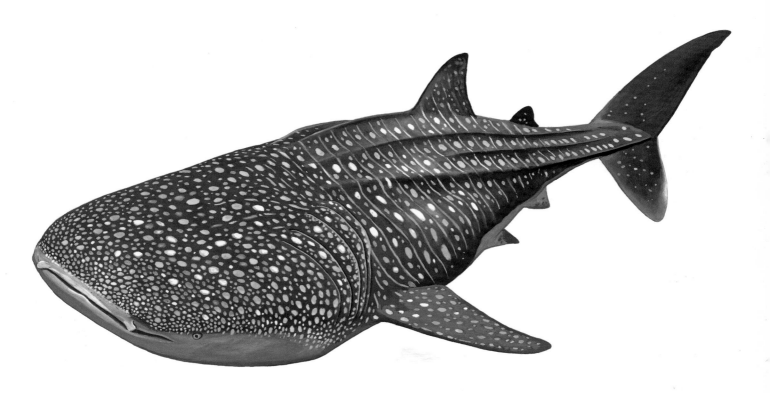

Oceans

The oceans form one huge, interconnected environment—a continuous layer of salt water that covers about three-quarters of the earth's surface. This ocean environment is very different from the familiar world of land and air that we live in, and the oceans have a different kind of geography.

Ocean climate

There is no weather in the underwater world, but there are different types of ocean "climate." Temperature is very important. In some respects, the oceans follow the global climate pattern, with cold water around the poles and the warmest water in the tropical regions. The depth of water is even more important. The Sun only warms the top few feet of water, just below the ocean surface. In deeper, darker waters, the temperature remains fairly constant.

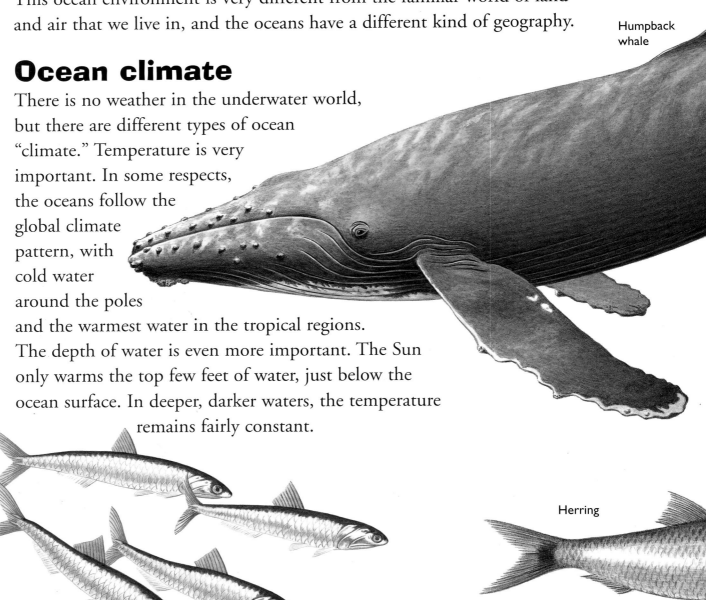

Humpback whale

Herring

Anchoveta

Deep water

Sunlight, as opposed to "sun-heat," has a slightly greater effect—down to a depth of about 300 feet (100 m). Below that depth, it is hard to tell whether it is day or night above the surface. The oceans extend to depths of more than 3,000 feet (1,000 m) and shallow water, less than 300 feet (100 m) in depth, is found only around the coasts of continents and islands. Some ocean trenches can be miles deep. In many ways, depth of water is more important to ocean life than geographical position.

Dragon fish

Familiar animals

The oceans have a greater variety of animal life than any other environment on Earth, although there are some familiar animal groups that are either present only in small numbers, or absent entirely. There are few mammals, and even fewer reptiles in the oceans. There are no amphibians, because they cannot tolerate salt water, and there are no insects. There are however large numbers of small animals with eyes and jointed legs—such as copepods, krill, and shrimp—that are related to insects.

Weddell seal

Ocean life

Copepod

The oceans permit a great variety of animals to follow ways of life that are not possible on land. The most simple way of life is to simply drift in the water and eat whatever comes close. Animals that live in this way are called plankton. Some animals spend their whole lives as plankton, while many others spend only the early part of their lives as plankton.

Krill

Fixed in place

Some animal groups have chosen a fixed way of life. Individuals attach themselves to a suitable surface and simply catch any plankton or other food that comes close enough. Corals, barnacles, and sea fans live in this way, and many worms and bivalve mollusks bury themselves in sand or mud. Most, but by no means all, of the creatures that live like this are found in shallow water.

Coral

West Indian sea fan

Moving about

Some ocean animals, such as starfish, urchins, and gastropod mollusks, walk or crawl over the seabed and rocks, but most animals prefer to swim. Fish are undoubtedly the best swimmers, because they do not have to come to the surface to breathe—like most ocean creatures, they obtain oxygen directly from seawater. But some air-breathers, such as dolphins, are just as quick and agile in the water.

Indo-Pacific humpbacked dolphin

Special places

The oceans have a number of regions where life is especially abundant. Coastlines, where the depth of water varies with the tides, are particularly important for seabirds. Coral reefs, which occur along some tropical coasts, have the richest and most colorful variety of animal life, but they are also the most delicate parts of the ocean environment. Near the poles, during winter, there is the unusual situation of the ocean depths being warmer than the ocean surface, and ocean life being much more abundant than life on land.

Little penguin

Aa

Max length: 4 inches (10 cm)

Acorn barnacle

The acorn barnacle is a small animal that is related to crabs and shrimp. Like other barnacles, it has a protective shell and is shaped like a volcano. The shell is kept closed at low tide. At high tide, feathery legs protrude from the top of the shell and catch plankton from the water. It lives attached to a surface such as a rock—or even the skin of a large fish or whale.

Fact

The acorn barnacle attaches itself directly to a surface, but some other barnacles attach themselves by a flexible stalk.

Max length: 8 inches (20 cm)

Anchoveta

This small, slim fish is related to anchovies and herring, which are found throughout the world's oceans. The anchoveta forms huge schools—of up to 20 million fish—in the cool waters off the western coast of South America. During the day, it swims at a depth of about 165 feet (50 m), but at night it comes within a few feet of the surface.

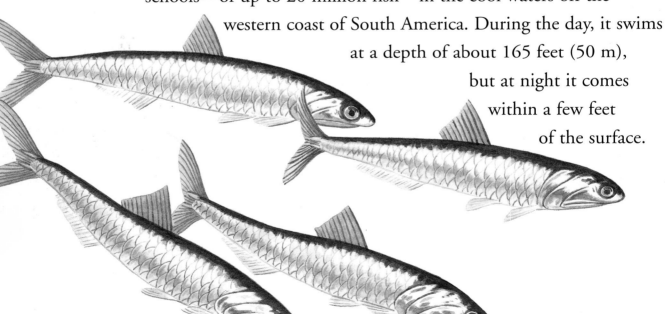

Angelshark

Max length: 5 feet (1.5 m)

The Pacific angelshark lives in shallow waters along the coasts of North and South America. It has a wide, flattened body and is often mistaken for a ray. Angelsharks, which are sometimes called monkfish, are ambush hunters. They wait on the sea bottom for their prey to come close enough to trap in their jaws.

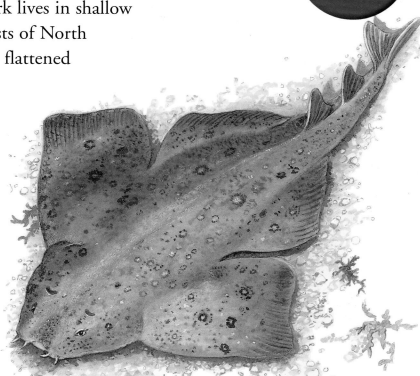

Atlantic cod

Max length: 4½ feet (1.4 m)

The cod is a long, slender fish that inhabits the cool waters around the edges of the North Atlantic. It prefers to stay about 165 feet (50 m) below the surface and forms schools in areas with a flat, sandy seabed. Atlantic cod have long lives and can weigh up to 200 lb (90 kg) when fully grown. Commercial fishing boats now catch most cod before they can grow to more than 33 lb (15 kg).

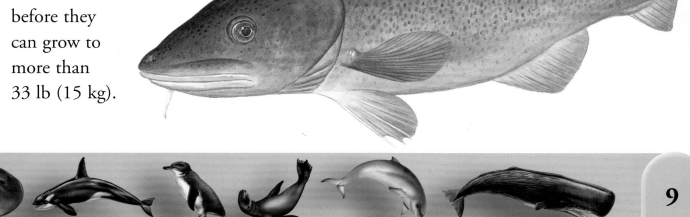

Aa Bb

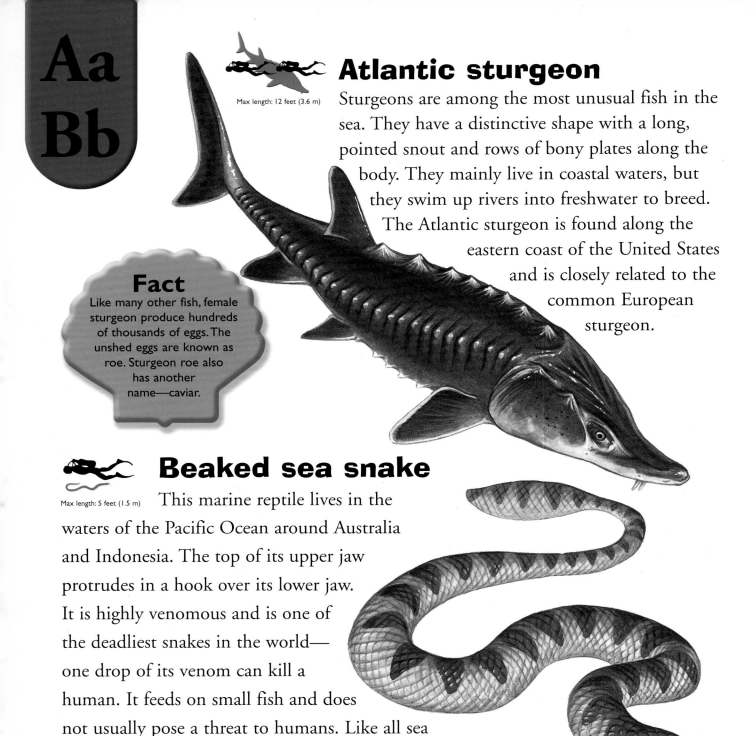

Max length: 12 feet (3.6 m)

Atlantic sturgeon

Sturgeons are among the most unusual fish in the sea. They have a distinctive shape with a long, pointed snout and rows of bony plates along the body. They mainly live in coastal waters, but they swim up rivers into freshwater to breed. The Atlantic sturgeon is found along the eastern coast of the United States and is closely related to the common European sturgeon.

Fact

Like many other fish, female sturgeon produce hundreds of thousands of eggs. The unshed eggs are known as roe. Sturgeon roe also has another name—caviar.

Beaked sea snake

Max length: 5 feet (1.5 m)

This marine reptile lives in the waters of the Pacific Ocean around Australia and Indonesia. The top of its upper jaw protrudes in a hook over its lower jaw. It is highly venomous and is one of the deadliest snakes in the world— one drop of its venom can kill a human. It feeds on small fish and does not usually pose a threat to humans. Like all sea snakes, it gives birth to live young instead of laying eggs.

Max length: 18 feet (5.5 m)

Beluga whale

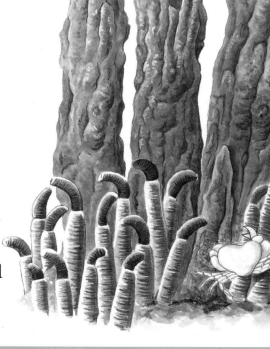

Also known as the white whale, this marine mammal is found only in the cold waters of the Arctic region. It is also known as the sea canary because of the variety of noises it makes. Belugas often gather in groups of more than 100 during the summer months. They spend a lot of time at the surface and are sometimes attacked by polar bears, although their main enemy is the killer whale.

Max height: 23 feet (7 m)

Black smoker

Black smokers are the deep-sea equivalent of hot springs. Cloudy, mineral-rich water streams out of vents in the ocean floor. The minerals give the water a very dark coloration and build up in jagged structures around the vents. Some unusual deep-sea animals live around black smokers, such as 10-foot (3-m) tall tubeworms, which are found nowhere else on Earth.

Bb

Max length: 2½ feet (81 cm)

Blue-footed booby

This seabird is related to pelicans, but it does not have a large pouch for storing fish. It is found mainly around the coasts of Central America, where it dives into the sea to catch fish such as sardines and mackerel. When diving down, it can reach speeds of 60 mph (100 km/h). The males are much smaller than the females and can dive into very shallow water such as rock pools.

Max length: 2 inches (5 cm)

Blue sea slug

This strange-looking gastropod mollusk is related to shellfish such as the conch. Despite its appearance, the blue sea slug does not have any legs. It has a single "foot" along the underside of its body like other gastropods. The leg-like flaps at the side of its body help it float upside-down just beneath the water's surface.

Fact
The blue sea slug is a predator that feeds on small jellyfish. It does not eat the jellyfish's stinging cells, but stores them inside its body as a defense weapon. It is immune to the stinging cells.

Max length: 12½ feet (3.8 m)

Blue shark

This large shark is a dangerous and aggressive predator. It usually stays away from land, but it sometimes visits coastal kelp beds. These are areas where a large amount of seaweed grows. Like many other sharks, the blue shark uses countershading to conceal its presence. This means the upper part of its body has a much darker coloration than the pale underside. This makes the animal difficult to spot either from above or below.

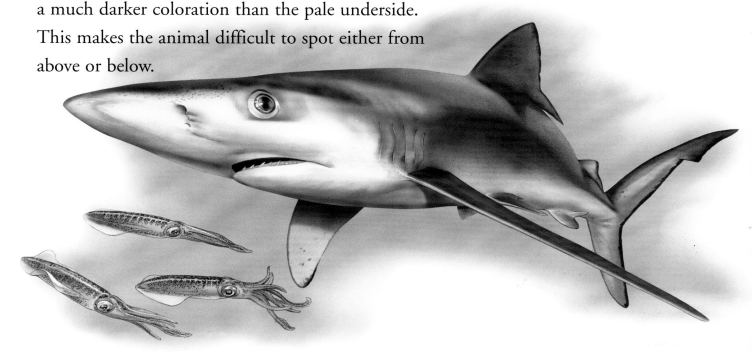

Max length: 3½ feet (105 cm)

Bonefish

This medium-sized fish is found in warm, coastal waters on both sides of the Atlantic Ocean. It feeds mainly on shellfish and other animals that live in the mud of the ocean floor. The bonefish uncovers its prey by swimming in a head-down position and blowing jets of water from its mouth to disturb the mud.

Cc

Max length: 5 inches (12 cm)

Cleaner wrasse

The cleaner wrasse is found on coral reefs. It feeds mainly on the parasites that infest the skin of other reef fish. Small groups of cleaner wrasse establish "cleaning stations" where the other fish circle in a "queue" while waiting for the wrasse to pick them clean of parasites.

Max length: 3½ inches (9 cm)

Clown anemone fish

This small fish gets its name from its bright colors, which resemble the face paint of a clown. It swims slowly, so it is an easy target for predators, but it spends most of its time hiding among the deadly tentacles of a sea anemone. Each tentacle of the sea anemone is tipped with venomous stinging cells that can easily kill other small fish, but the clown anemone fish is immune to this venom.

Max length: 8 inches (20 cm)

Comet

The comet is a small fish with a very clever means of defense. When a predator appears, the comet sticks its head into a rock or cave—and does nothing. The shape of its fins, and the distinctive "eye-spot" marking, make the half-hidden fish look just like the head of a fearsome species of moray eel.

Max length: 8 feet (2.4 m)

Common dolphin

The common dolphin is one of the most widespread of all marine mammals. It is found in the warmer parts of the world's seas and oceans. There are two sub-species of the common dolphin—long-beaked and short-beaked. Both sub-species have yellowish patches on their sides that distinguish them from other kinds of dolphins. Although sometimes seen in coastal waters, the common dolphin prefers the open sea far away from land.

Max length: ⅙ inch (4 mm)

Fact
Copepods, together with shrimp, crabs, and lobsters, are crustaceans. Unlike the other members of this group, copepods do not have a hardened outer casing.

Copepod

There are about 12,000 species of copepods. These tiny shrimp-like creatures are part of the plankton that feed millions of ocean animals. Copepods feed on smaller animals and tiny floating plants. When food is plentiful, copepods are seen in swarms containing billions of individuals.

Cc Coral

A coral animal (also called a polyp) is like a tiny sea anemone. It lives attached to a surface and catches food with stinging tentacles. Most coral animals make a protective stony cup for themselves from the minerals in seawater. These cups build up in layers to form a variety of stony shapes covered by a living layer of coral animals. Over time, corals build up into a ridge of rock called a coral reef.

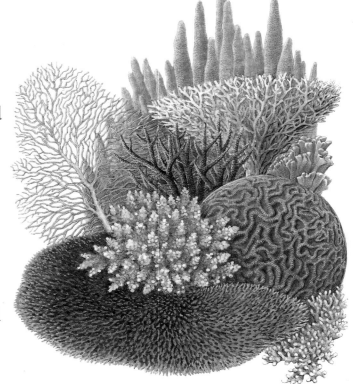

Fact
All corals consist of colonies of tiny polyps. Hard corals (or stony corals) build reefs. Soft corals, such as sea pens and sea lilies, live on reefs but do not help build them.

Max length: 2½ feet (80 cm)

Crown-of-thorns

The crown-of-thorns starfish (or sea star) has become a major pest on some coral reefs. All starfish are predators and most feed on crabs and sea urchins that they pull apart with their sucker-lined arms. The crown-of-thorns specializes in eating coral polyps, and these starfish are seen in such large numbers that they can eat a whole reef.

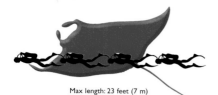

Max length: 23 feet (7 m)

Devilfish

The devilfish has a fearsome appearance, but like its close relative the manta ray, it is harmless to humans. It swims by slowly flapping its enormous "wings," and feeds mainly on small fish. This huge ray is found only in the warmer parts of the eastern Atlantic Ocean.

Dragon fish

Max length: 22 inches (55 cm)

This deepwater predator has a long, thin body like an eel. The dragon fish feeds at night and moves from the depths of the water to nearer the surface. It attracts prey in the darkness of the ocean depths with small patches along the underside of its body that send out light. It also has a larger light organ that dangles beneath its wide jaw, which is full of sharp, pointed teeth.

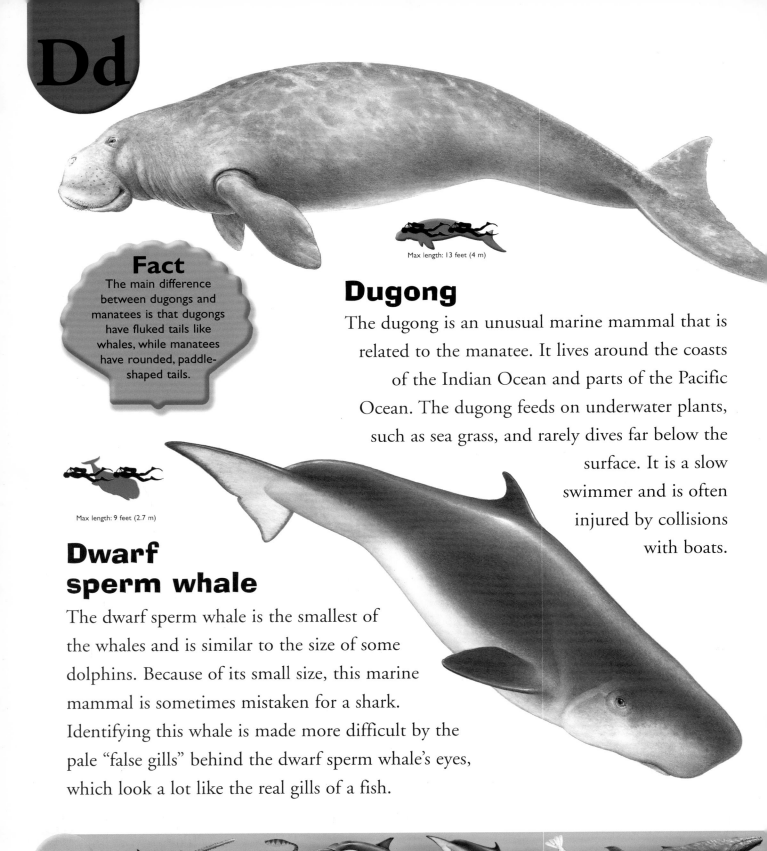

Dd

Fact

The main difference between dugongs and manatees is that dugongs have fluked tails like whales, while manatees have rounded, paddle-shaped tails.

Max length: 13 feet (4 m)

Dugong

The dugong is an unusual marine mammal that is related to the manatee. It lives around the coasts of the Indian Ocean and parts of the Pacific Ocean. The dugong feeds on underwater plants, such as sea grass, and rarely dives far below the surface. It is a slow swimmer and is often injured by collisions with boats.

Max length: 9 feet (2.7 m)

Dwarf sperm whale

The dwarf sperm whale is the smallest of the whales and is similar to the size of some dolphins. Because of its small size, this marine mammal is sometimes mistaken for a shark. Identifying this whale is made more difficult by the pale "false gills" behind the dwarf sperm whale's eyes, which look a lot like the real gills of a fish.

Elephant seal

Max length: 21 feet (6.5 m)

This marine mammal lives in the cool waters around Antarctica. Male elephant seals, which are four times heavier than the females, are the largest of all seals. Although they are clumsy on land, these mammals are superb swimmers and can dive to a depth of 1,970 feet (600 m) in search of their favorite food, which is squid.

Emperor penguin

Max height: 3½ feet (110 cm)

Emperor penguins live around the coast of Antarctica. These birds have become famous because of their devotion to their eggs. After the female has laid an egg, the male spends several months standing on the ice keeping the egg warm, without feeding even once.

Emperor shrimp

Max length: ¼ inch (2 cm)

This small shrimp is found on coral reefs. It lives mainly on and around sea cucumbers (larger soft-bodied animals) and sea slugs. The emperor shrimp hides from predators beneath the sea cucumber. In return, the shrimp acts as a cleaner and keeps its protector free from skin parasites. The shrimp's color varies depending on the animal on which it is living.

Fact
Sea cucumbers are soft, sausage-shaped animals that are related to sea urchins and starfish. They can grow to more than 3 feet (100 cm) in length.

Flamingo, greater

Max length: 4¾ feet (145 cm)

The greater flamingo lives mainly around the coastlines of the Caribbean Sea and the Indian Ocean. It prefers wide, muddy areas and lagoons. Although the greater flamingo mainly feeds while wading in the shallows, it is a good swimmer and sometimes bobs underwater like a duck. Flamingos that live around the Caribbean are bright pink, but those around the Indian Ocean are noticeably paler.

Flying gurnard

Max length: 15 inches (38 cm)

This unusual fish does not fly, but it uses its extraordinary "wings" to walk across the ocean floor. The flying gurnard lives in the warmer parts of the Atlantic Ocean and feeds mainly on shellfish and other animals buried in undersea mud. The fish's "wings" are actually greatly enlarged fins that can be extended like a semicircular cloak.

Frilled shark

Max length: 6½ feet (2 m)

This unusual shark is also known as the eel-shark because of its long, slim shape. It gets its name from the frills of skin along the gills on the sides of its head. The frilled shark lives mainly in deep water and rarely comes to the surface. It has small, pointed teeth and feeds mostly on squid.

Ff Gg

Frogfish

Max length: 4½ inches (11.5 cm)

The roughbar frogfish lives along the warmer coasts of the eastern Pacific Ocean. Although it is related to the deep-sea anglerfish, the frogfish is generally found in fairly shallow waters. It feeds mainly on crabs and shrimp on the seabed, but will also attack fish as large as itself.

Giant squid

Nobody is sure just how big giant squid can grow. These mysterious animals live in deep water, far away from land and are never seen at the surface. Apart from a few images captured by underwater cameras, scientists have to rely on studying the bodies of giant squid that are occasionally washed up on shore.

Max length: 65½ feet (20 m)

Max length: 26 feet (8 m)

Great white shark

This large fish has a fearsome reputation that is well deserved. The great white shark is one of the largest predators in the oceans and has no natural enemies. It is normally found in the open oceans, but is sometimes sighted in coastal waters. The great white shark has been known to attack humans and small boats.

Max length: 20 inches (50 cm)

Guinea fowl puffer

This puffer fish lives in shallow waters around coral reefs across the Indian and Pacific oceans. Like other puffer fish, it has a soft, semi-shapeless body. When danger threatens, it can inflate its body to almost twice its normal width, making prickly spines stand out from its skin.

Gg
Hh

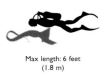

Max length: 6 feet
(1.8 m)

Gulper eel

The gulper eel lives in deep tropical waters. It has huge jaws and an expandable stomach, which means it can eat prey much larger than itself. The gulper eel is poorly designed for chasing after prey—instead, it is believed to collect food by swimming slowly with its mouth open. It has a patch on the end of its tail that sends out light to attract prey.

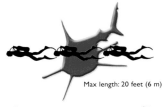

Max length: 20 feet (6 m)

Hammerhead shark

This unusual shark has a peculiar T-shaped head. Its eyes are located wide apart at the ends of the T. Like most other sharks, the hammerhead is a fierce predator. It uses its razor-sharp teeth to slice great chunks of flesh from its prey.

Max length: 5 inches (12 cm)

Harlequin ghost pipefish

This small fish is related to seahorses and sea dragons. Its bright coloration and feathery fins make it difficult for predators to see among the exotic colors and shapes on the coral reefs of the Pacific Ocean.

Fact

The female ghost pipefish uses the large fins on her stomach to form a pouch. The eggs are protected in this pouch until they hatch.

Max length: 5½ feet (1.7 m)

Harp seal

The harp seal is found near the edges of the sea ice around Greenland and in the Arctic Ocean. This marine mammal dives deep underwater in search of fish such as cod. It can hold its breath for more than 15 minutes. Harp seals live in groups of several hundred animals.

Fact

The harp seal gets its name from the dark, curved shapes in the fur on its back. On some animals these shapes join up to look just like a harp.

Hh

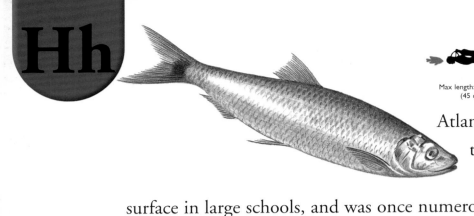

Herring

Max length: 18 inches (45 cm)

The sleek and silvery Atlantic herring is a close relative of the anchoveta. It swims in both deeper water and near the surface in large schools, and was once numerous in the seas around northern Europe. There are now fewer herring because of modern fishing methods, and so commercial fishing has become more strictly controlled to protect them.

Herring gull

Max length: 24 inches (60 cm)

The herring gull is the most widespread seabird around the coasts of North America, Europe, and northern Asia. Its numbers are increasing rapidly because it has adapted to living alongside humans. Instead of their natural diet of fish, such as herring, many of these gulls now feed at waste dumps and landfill sites.

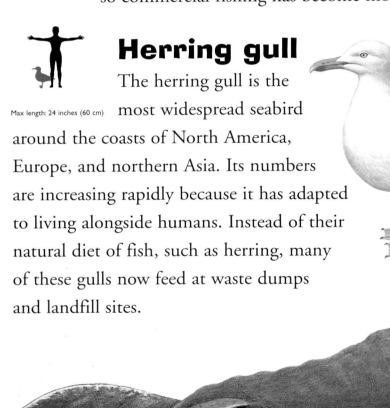

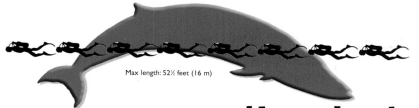

Max length: 52½ feet (16 m)

Humpback whale

This large marine mammal is found in all but the very coldest parts of the oceans. It is often seen at the surface and can be recognized by its long flippers and knobbly head. Its head may also be covered with barnacles. Humpback whales migrate long distances across the oceans, moving to warmer waters in time for their summer breeding season.

Max length: 16½ inches (42 cm)

Inca tern

This seabird lives along the western coast of South America. It is easily recognizable by the white "moustache" feathers on either side of its beak. The Inca tern dives into the sea to catch small fish such as the anchoveta. Large numbers of these birds often gather above feeding humpback whales. They wait to dive for any scraps the whales may leave.

Ii Jj

Max length: 9 feet
(2.8 m)

Indo-Pacific humpbacked dolphin

This marine mammal prefers shallow coastal waters and is rarely seen far from land. It feeds on small fish, especially around the edges of swamps. The size of the hump in the middle of its back varies from animal to animal, and on some it is hardly noticeable. The coloration may also vary, from greenish, to brown, to blue-gray.

Max length: 10 inches (26 cm)

Jack knifefish

This small fish is easily recognized by the long fin behind its head. It lives in the Caribbean Sea and around the northern coast of South America. The jack knifefish belongs to a group of fish that are often called "drummers." By flexing special muscles inside its body, it can make sounds that can be heard by humans swimming nearby.

Japanese giant spider crab

Max length: 12 feet (3.7 m)

This is by far the largest crustacean, although most of its size is in its outstretched and elongated legs. Its actual body is much smaller than some lobsters. The Japanese giant spider crab lives in deep water in the northwest Pacific Ocean. Like other crabs, it feeds mainly on dead fish and other creatures that sink to the ocean floor.

Max length: 26 inches (66 cm)

John Dory

The John Dory is found in deep waters around the coasts of Europe, Africa, and Australia. It is very narrow with an unusually large head that accounts for about one third of the total length of its body and has large spiny fins. The John Dory is a solitary fish that does not swim in schools. It feeds on fish and crabs, which it hunts near the seabed.

Kk

Max length: 33 feet (10 m)

Killer whale

Despite its name, this marine mammal is more closely related to dolphins than to true whales. The killer whale is found throughout the seas and oceans, but especially in polar regions. It lives in family groups of about ten to 20 animals, which are known as pods. They feed mainly on fish such as salmon and tuna.

Fact
Toothed whales such as the killer whale feed on creatures like fish and squid. They find prey using echolocation—the animals send out sounds and use the echoes to locate their prey.

Max length: 24 inches (60 cm)

King crab

Also known as the horseshoe crab, the king crab is one of the strangest creatures in the sea. It is not a true crab—its nearest living relatives are spiders and scorpions. King crabs live in much the same way as true crabs and prefer sheltered, sandy beaches along the eastern coasts of North America and Asia. They feed on worms and mollusks living in mud.

Krill

Max length: 1½ inches (4 cm)

Krill are small animals that are closely related to shrimp. In addition to forming part of the general plankton, krill can form huge swarms that weigh more than two billions pounds (one billion kilograms). The swarms of krill in Arctic and Antarctic waters are a major source of food for whales such as the humpback and the blue whale.

Laced moray

Max length: 10 feet (3 m)

The laced moray is one of about 200 species of moray eels that live on coral reefs around the world. Morays spend most of the day crammed into narrow crevices in the coral and come out at night to feed. They have wide jaws with rows of sharp teeth, which they use to grab hold of squid and small fish.

Ll

Max length: 2½ inches (6 cm)

Lancelet

This small, slim marine animal is not a fish or any other sort of sea creature. The 24 species of lancelets that live in warm, shallow waters around the world are in a group of their own. Lancelets can swim by flexing their bodies from side to side, but they spend most of their time buried in sand and gravel with only their heads sticking out.

Fact

The lancelet is interesting to scientists because it is the nearest thing to a vertebrate (an animal with a backbone) that does not actually have a backbone.

Leopard seal

Max length: 11½ feet (3.5 m)

The leopard seal is a fierce predator that will attack and eat seabirds and other seals as well as fish and squid. Penguins are also an important part of its diet. This marine mammal lives in the cold waters around Antarctica. Leopard seals often wait underwater to ambush penguins coming back to shore.

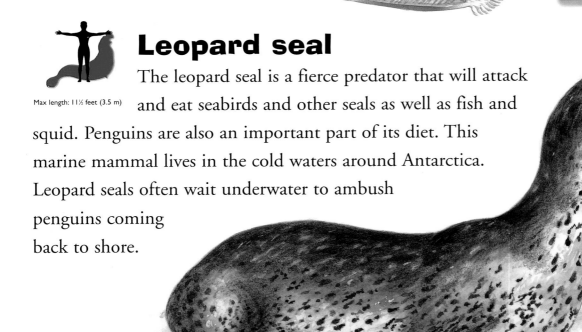

Lesser beaked whale

Max length: 12 feet (3.7 m)

The lesser beaked whale is the smallest of the beaked whales. It was not discovered until 1991. It lives in very deep water off the eastern coast of Peru, and is only very rarely seen at the surface. The lesser beaked whale has only two tiny teeth in its lower jaw. Scientists believe that it mainly feeds on squid that it swallows whole.

Fact
Although they breathe air like other whales and dolphins, beaked whales spend much less time at the surface than their marine mammal relatives.

Max height: 18 inches (45 cm)

Little penguin

This is the smallest of the penguins and it is found only around the coasts of New Zealand and southern Australia. It usually nests in burrows, caves, and under rocks, although it has also been found nesting under seaside houses. It spends all day out at sea in search of food and only returns to land after sunset.

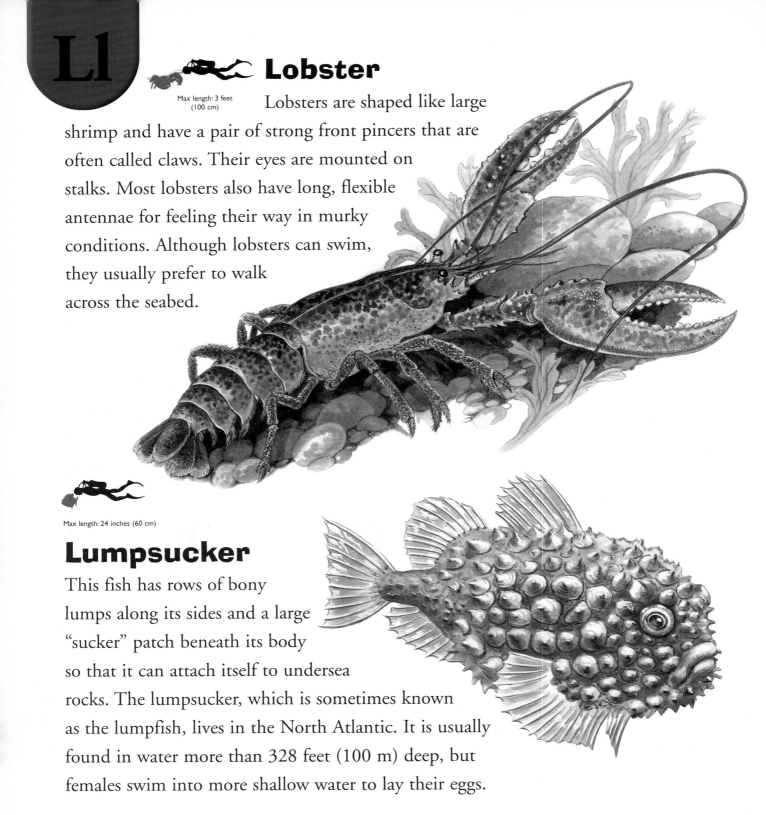

Lobster

Max length: 3 feet (100 cm)

Lobsters are shaped like large shrimp and have a pair of strong front pincers that are often called claws. Their eyes are mounted on stalks. Most lobsters also have long, flexible antennae for feeling their way in murky conditions. Although lobsters can swim, they usually prefer to walk across the seabed.

Max length: 24 inches (60 cm)

Lumpsucker

This fish has rows of bony lumps along its sides and a large "sucker" patch beneath its body so that it can attach itself to undersea rocks. The lumpsucker, which is sometimes known as the lumpfish, lives in the North Atlantic. It is usually found in water more than 328 feet (100 m) deep, but females swim into more shallow water to lay their eggs.

Mackerel

The Atlantic mackerel is a sleek predator that feeds mainly on young fish and shrimp. It forms large schools that are an attractive target for other predators. Mackerel often swim close to the surface. The patterns on their upper sides make individual mackerel a more difficult target for diving seabirds.

Max length: 24 inches (60 cm)

Marine iguana

Max length: 3 feet (100 cm)

The marine iguana is the only lizard that swims in the sea. These reptiles live only around the coast of the Galapagos Islands in the eastern Pacific Ocean. They can dive 40 feet (12 m) down to feed on underwater plants and can stay underwater for up to one hour. They then climb up onto rocks to warm up in the sun.

Mm

Max length: 1 inch (2.5 cm)

Mottled red chiton

This unusual mollusk is found on rocky shores around the coasts of Britain and eastern Canada. Instead of having one or two shells like most other mollusks, the chiton's shell is made up of eight overlapping pieces. It clings to rocks and feeds on microscopic plants.

Fact

When out of water, mudskippers can breathe by absorbing oxygen through their skin in the same way as some amphibians.

Mudskipper

Max length: 10 inches (26 cm)

The mudskipper is an unusual fish that is as much at home on land as in the water. It lives in tidal, tropical swamps around the coasts of Africa and Southeast Asia. When the tide goes out, mudskippers move around on land and even climb trees, using their strong front fins. Their eyes can be rolled back in their sockets to keep them moist.

Murre

Max length: 14 inches (36 cm)

The murre is a common seabird around the coasts of the north Atlantic. It floats on the water like a duck and then dives below the surface for up to one minute to chase fish. Murres do not build any sort of nest, but lay their eggs on narrow cliff ledges. The eggs are pear-shaped so that they roll around in a circle instead of rolling off the ledge.

Musky octopus

Max length: 24 inches (60 cm)

Octopuses are mollusks that are related to gastropod and bivalve shellfish. Although they can swim by squirting out jets of water to push themselves along, they prefer to clamber over underwater surfaces using their flexible tentacles. The musky octopus lives around the coast of the northwest Atlantic and the Mediterranean Sea.

Nn

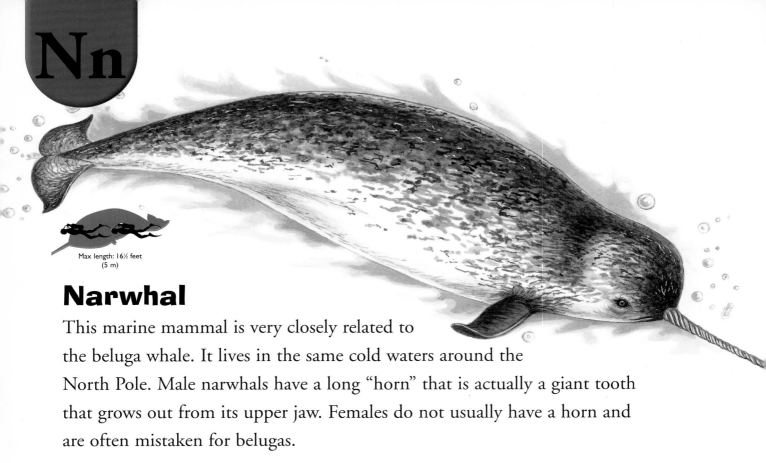

Max length: 16½ feet
(5 m)

Narwhal

This marine mammal is very closely related to
the beluga whale. It lives in the same cold waters around the
North Pole. Male narwhals have a long "horn" that is actually a giant tooth
that grows out from its upper jaw. Females do not usually have a horn and
are often mistaken for belugas.

Nautilus

Max length: 8 inches (20 cm)

The nautilus is another of the ocean's many
oddities. This mollusk is distantly related to
squid, but is much more closely related to
animals that died out many millions
of years ago. The nautilus has hollow
chambers inside its shell that
allow it to drift "weightlessly"
at a particular depth. It catches
small fish and shrimp with
its tentacles.

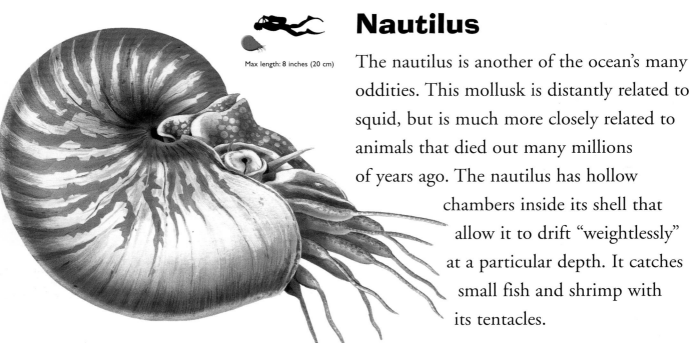

Max length: 3 feet (100 cm)

Neptune's cup

Neptune's cup is one of more than 9,000 species of sponge. Sponges live attached to a solid surface, and are especially common on coral reefs. A sponge is the simplest form of multi-celled animal. It has no digestive system and no nervous system. It absorbs microscopic food particles directly from water, which flows through the many holes in its body structure.

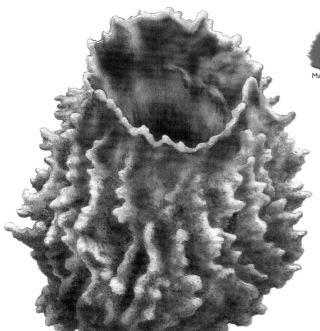

Max length: 14 feet (4.3 m)

Nurse shark

This shark lives around coral reefs in the warmer parts of the Atlantic and eastern Pacific oceans. It spends the day hiding in shadows and comes out mainly at night. It is a sluggish swimmer and feeds on slow-moving prey such as lobsters, octopuses, and other mollusks.

Oo

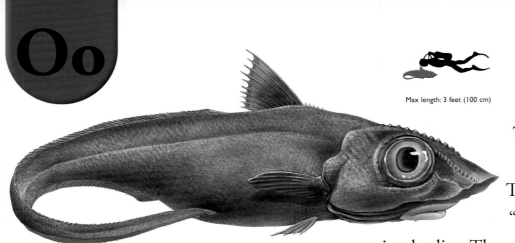

Max length: 3 feet (100 cm)

Onion-eyed grenadier

There are more than 300 species of grenadiers. These fish are often called "rat-tails" because of their tapering bodies. The onion-eyed grenadier lives on the ocean floor around the edges of the Atlantic Ocean. Its large eyes help it find food such as shellfish and worms.

Max length: 6 feet (1.8 m)

Opah

This large fish prefers deep water away from land, and is found in all but the coldest waters. The opah is also known as the moonfish because of its shape and its silvery-blue color when viewed from the surface. This fish does not flex its body to swim, but uses its narrow side fins to "fly" through the water after prey such as squid.

Max length: 24 inches (60 cm)

Orange roughy

The orange roughy lives in the Atlantic and Indian oceans and around the coast of Australia. It prefers deep water near the ocean floor where its orange color appears darker and helps to hide it from predators.

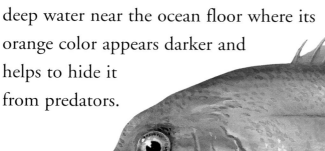

Max length: 2½ feet (81 cm)

Oriental sweetlips

This brightly colored fish is found near patches of sand around the coral reefs of Southeast Asia. It gets its name from its soft mouth that helps it to "vacuum" up worms and other animals that live in the sand. When it is feeding, a telltale cloud of sand is "blown" out of its gills. It can produce sounds by grinding the teeth at the rear of its mouth.

Max length: 23 inches (58 cm)

Osprey

This bird of prey is found around the coastlines of every continent except Antarctica. The osprey is often called a "fish eagle," although this name actually belongs to another bird. The osprey catches fish by diving into water feet first and grabbing its prey in special non-slip talons (claws).

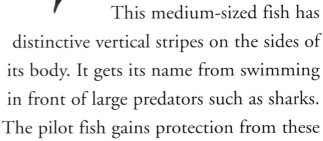

Max length: 17 inches (43 cm)

Oystercatcher

The oystercatcher is a familiar sight around the shores of Europe. It is a wading bird that feeds mainly on bivalve mollusks. This bird has two ways of opening these shellfish. It either uses its beak to snip the muscle holding the two valves together, or it simply picks the shellfish up and smashes it against a rock.

Max length: 27½ inches (70 cm)

Pilot fish

This medium-sized fish has distinctive vertical stripes on the sides of its body. It gets its name from swimming in front of large predators such as sharks. The pilot fish gains protection from these fierce companions. In return, it eats any parasites that may attach themselves to the sharks' skin.

Max length: 1½ inches (4 cm)

Plankton

Plankton is the name given to the tiny plants and animals that provide food for many of the ocean's larger inhabitants. Some animals, such as copepods, remain part of the plankton for their whole lives. With many others, including fish, crabs, coral, and starfish, it is just the larval (young) forms that are part of the plankton—the adults are often plankton-eaters.

Fact

The tiny plants in plankton are called phytoplankton. The tiny animals are called zooplankton.

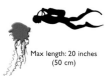

Max length: 20 inches (50 cm)

Portuguese man-of-war

This large jellyfish has a gas-filled "sail" that keeps it floating on the water's surface. The long streamers that hang down from its body can reach 65½ feet (20 m) in length. These streamers are covered with stinging cells that contain venom strong enough to kill small fish.

Pp

Max length: 12 inches (30 cm)

Prickly leatherjacket

Also known as the leafy filefish, this animal lives on the coral reefs of the Indian and western Pacific oceans. It has tassels of skin to help it hide from predators among strands of seaweed. This fish also has another form of defense—a strong spine on the top of its head. This spine lies flat unless predators come close by.

Puffin

The Atlantic puffin is easily recognizable by its large multicolored beak. This seabird likes to live in large groups called colonies that are often located on the tops of rocky cliffs. At sea, puffins sometimes form floating "rafts" of hundreds of birds as they wait for a school of herring or other small fish to swim beneath them.

Max length: 12½ inches (32 cm)

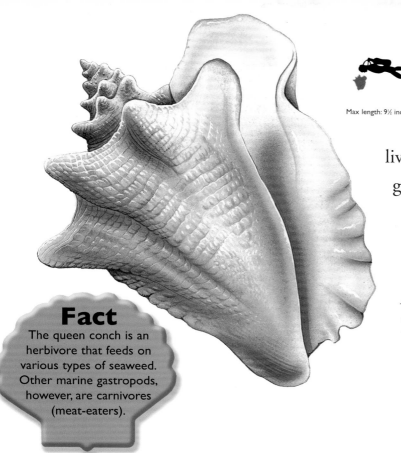

Queen conch

Qq

Max length: 9½ inches (24 cm)

This large gastropod mollusk lives in the Caribbean Sea. When fully grown, it can weigh 2¼ lb (1 kg). It is now a protected species because so many people have collected it for food and for its magnificent shell. All conches have a distinctive flaring lip around the shell opening; but on the queen conch, the lip curls over and flares outward.

Fact

The queen conch is an herbivore that feeds on various types of seaweed. Other marine gastropods, however, are carnivores (meat-eaters).

Queensland grouper

Max length: 9 feet (2.7 m)

This large, heavy fish lives around the reefs of the Indian and Pacific oceans. It does not like open water, but prefers to stay close to the coral. Although it feeds mainly on crustaceans and shellfish, this grouper is one of the few reef-dwellers able to take on predators such as reef sharks and moray eels.

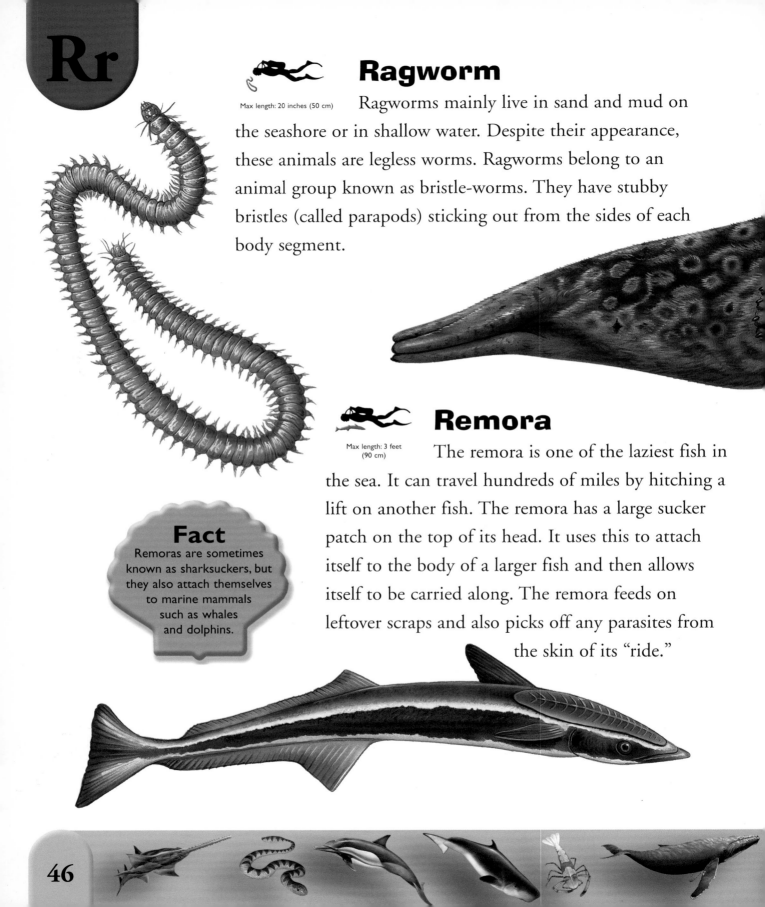

Rr

Ragworm

Max length: 20 inches (50 cm)

Ragworms mainly live in sand and mud on the seashore or in shallow water. Despite their appearance, these animals are legless worms. Ragworms belong to an animal group known as bristle-worms. They have stubby bristles (called parapods) sticking out from the sides of each body segment.

Remora

Max length: 3 feet (90 cm)

The remora is one of the laziest fish in the sea. It can travel hundreds of miles by hitching a lift on another fish. The remora has a large sucker patch on the top of its head. It uses this to attach itself to the body of a larger fish and then allows itself to be carried along. The remora feeds on leftover scraps and also picks off any parasites from the skin of its "ride."

Fact
Remoras are sometimes known as sharksuckers, but they also attach themselves to marine mammals such as whales and dolphins.

Ringed seal

Max length: 6 feet (1.8 m)

This species of seal is unusual because it lives in both salt water and freshwater. Most ringed seals live in the cold waters around the northern coasts of Europe and Asia. However, there are also ringed seals living happily in two freshwater lakes in Russia.

Fact
Risso's dolphin is highly unusual because it has a unique vertical crease down its forehead between its blowhole and mouth.

Risso's dolphin

Max length: 12½ feet (3.8 m)

This large dolphin is most often seen near remote mid-ocean islands and rarely comes close to the coasts of the continents. It has a distinctive rounded head and its gray skin is usually covered with white scars. Risso's dolphin is also known as the gray dolphin and it is sometimes called a grampus.

Max length: 3 feet (85 cm)

Salmon

The sockeye salmon is one of several salmon species that share an unusual lifestyle. Young salmon hatch from eggs in freshwater and then swim downriver to the sea. After a few years of ocean life, they return to the same stretch of freshwater, swimming up rivers and leaping up waterfalls to get there.

Fact
The saw-like snout of the sawfish is shaped like a flattened blade. The snout can be more than 3 feet (100 cm) in length and contains more than 50 teeth.

Max length: 25 feet (7.6 m)

Sawfish

The sawfish is a large predator that is related to skates and rays. It lives in warm coastal waters and feeds on schools of small fish that it slashes apart with its spiky-toothed snout. Sawfish are often confused with sawsharks, which look similar but are smaller.

Sea lion

Max length: 10 feet (3 m)

This marine mammal lives up to its name. It is a fierce predator that feeds on fish, seabirds, and seals. It can dive down to nearly 328 feet (100 m) in search of herring, but is more likely to find its prey closer to the surface. The sea lion looks similar to the seal, but can move about better on land. It can also swim at high speeds.

Sea otter

Max length: 4 feet (1.3 m)

The sea otter is the only member of the otter group that is a sea animal. Other otters may sometimes feed along the seashore, but the sea otter spends all of its time at sea. It eats clams while floating on its back—it rests a stone on its stomach and smashes a clam onto the stone to break the shell. The sea otter lives around parts of the north Pacific Ocean and feeds mainly on shellfish in offshore kelp beds.

Max length: 50 feet
(15 m)

Sei whale

This large marine mammal is found everywhere except the coldest polar waters. The sei whale feeds on zooplankton, which it filters from seawater with baleen plates inside its mouth. Sei whales usually live in groups of two to five animals but may form larger groups in areas where food is plentiful.

Max length: 9 feet (2.8 m)

Skate

Skates are small to medium-sized rays that live on the ocean floor in deep water, where they feed on shellfish and crustaceans. The so-called common skate was once numerous around the coasts of Europe, but numbers have recently declined because of over-fishing.

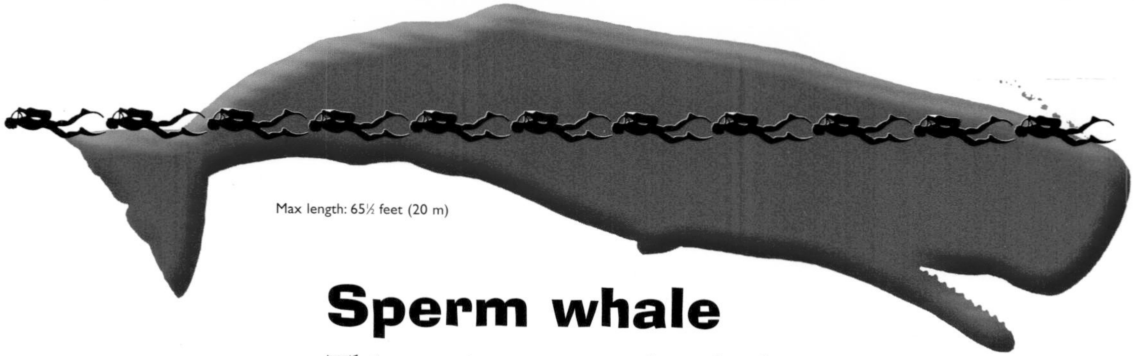

Max length: 65½ feet (20 m)

Sperm whale

This marine mammal is the largest of the toothed whales—as opposed to baleen whales like the humpback. It is found in all but the coldest parts of the oceans. Sperm whales dive to depths of up to 1¼ miles (2 km) in search of squid, which are their favorite food. They can remain underwater for up to two hours.

Tarpon

Max length: 8 feet (2.5 m)

This large fish lives in the coastal waters of the Atlantic Ocean. It can tolerate freshwater and is often found where rivers open into the ocean. The tarpon is a powerful predator that feeds on schools of smaller fish such as sardines and herring.

Tt

Max length: 24 feet (7.4 m)

Tiger shark

This large predator is found in warm tropical waters, usually at some distance from the coast. Equipped with rows of sharp, triangular teeth, the tiger shark is large enough to attack and kill just about any other sea creature. The dark markings on its upper side get paler as the shark gets older.

Torpedo

Max height: 6 feet (1.8 m)

The great torpedo ray is the largest member of a group known as the electric rays because they can deliver a powerful electric shock. The electricity is produced and stored in special muscles at the sides of their bodies. The torpedo lives on the ocean floor in the cooler parts of the Atlantic Ocean.

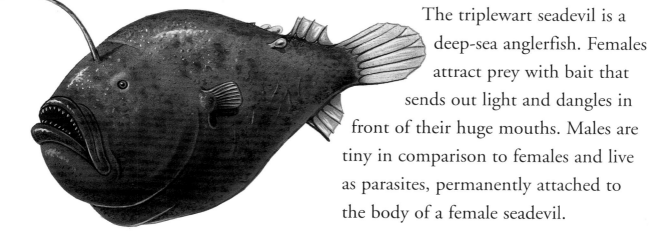

Max length: 3¼ feet (1 m)

Triplewart seadevil

The triplewart seadevil is a deep-sea anglerfish. Females attract prey with bait that sends out light and dangles in front of their huge mouths. Males are tiny in comparison to females and live as parasites, permanently attached to the body of a female seadevil.

Max length: 14 inches (36 cm)

Tripod fish

This ocean-floor predator waits patiently for any unsuspecting prey to come close. Food is in short supply at the bottom of the ocean and the tripod fish often waits for long periods of time before it is able to eat. It conserves energy by "standing" upright on its specially shaped fins, instead of having to use swimming muscles to hold itself in position.

Fact

The tripod fish has very poor eyesight. Scientists believe that it uses the fins behind its gills as sensors to detect the approach of prey.

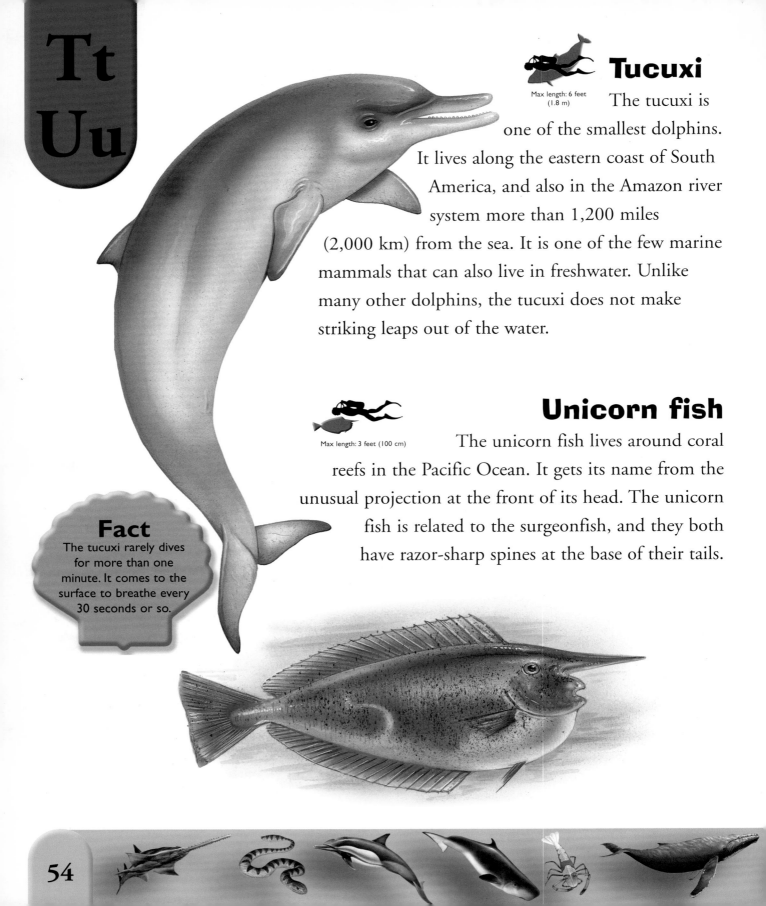

Tt
Uu

Tucuxi

Max length: 6 feet (1.8 m)

The tucuxi is one of the smallest dolphins. It lives along the eastern coast of South America, and also in the Amazon river system more than 1,200 miles (2,000 km) from the sea. It is one of the few marine mammals that can also live in freshwater. Unlike many other dolphins, the tucuxi does not make striking leaps out of the water.

Fact
The tucuxi rarely dives for more than one minute. It comes to the surface to breathe every 30 seconds or so.

Unicorn fish

Max length: 3 feet (100 cm)

The unicorn fish lives around coral reefs in the Pacific Ocean. It gets its name from the unusual projection at the front of its head. The unicorn fish is related to the surgeonfish, and they both have razor-sharp spines at the base of their tails.

Vampire squid

Max length: 2 inches (5 cm)

This small deep-sea mollusk has eight swimming tentacles, which are linked by webs of skin. It also has two additional feeding tentacles for grabbing prey. When threatened, the vampire squid enfolds itself in its webbed tentacles revealing sharp spines underneath.

Veiled angelmouth

Max length: 3 inches (7.6 cm)

This deep-sea predator lives in complete darkness. During the day, it stays too deep for any sunlight to reach and only rises closer to the surface at night. It has two rows of patches that send out light along each side of its body. These spots of light attract prey within range of the angelmouth's huge jaws.

Velvet whalefish

Max length: 14 inches (35 cm)

This small deep-sea fish got its name from its shape, not its size. Whalefish have poor eyesight because there is very little light at the depth where they live. Instead, they rely on a row of sensors along their sides to alert them to the presence of predators or prey.

Ww

Max length: 5½ feet (1.7 m)

Wahoo

This long, slim fish is one of the fastest swimmers in the sea. The wahoo is a fierce predator with a large mouth and strong teeth with sharp, serrated edges. When chasing after smaller prey, a wahoo can swim at a speed of more than 43 mph (70 km/h) for short periods of time.

Max length: 13 feet (4 m)

Walrus

This mammal is closely related to seals and sea lions. It lives in the cold waters of the Arctic and feeds on slow-moving prey that it searches for on the ocean floor. The long tusks of the male walrus are elongated upper teeth that are used for fighting with other males.

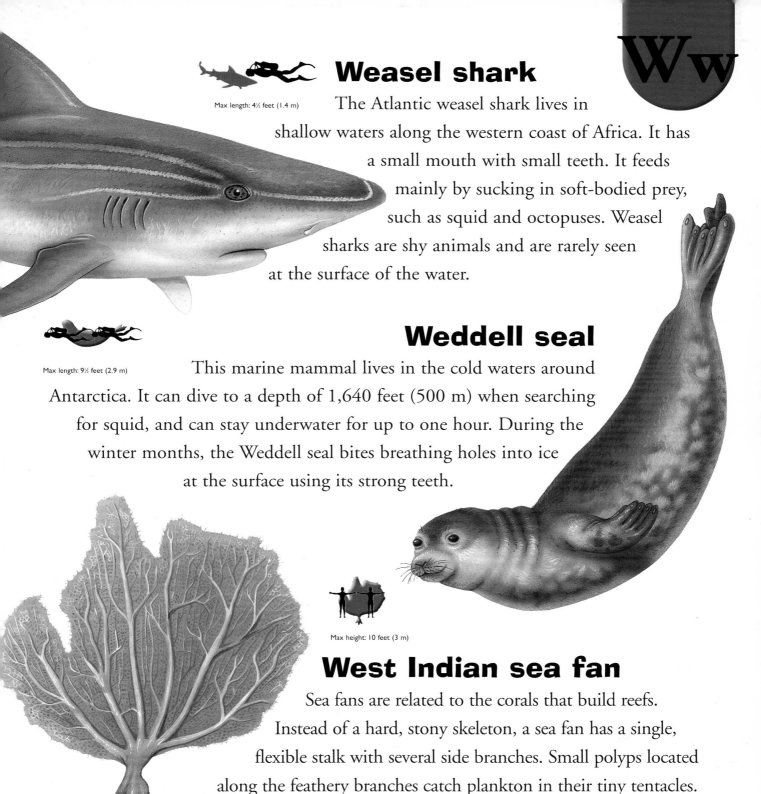

Weasel shark

Max length: 4½ feet (1.4 m)

The Atlantic weasel shark lives in shallow waters along the western coast of Africa. It has a small mouth with small teeth. It feeds mainly by sucking in soft-bodied prey, such as squid and octopuses. Weasel sharks are shy animals and are rarely seen at the surface of the water.

Weddell seal

Max length: 9½ feet (2.9 m)

This marine mammal lives in the cold waters around Antarctica. It can dive to a depth of 1,640 feet (500 m) when searching for squid, and can stay underwater for up to one hour. During the winter months, the Weddell seal bites breathing holes into ice at the surface using its strong teeth.

Max height: 10 feet (3 m)

West Indian sea fan

Sea fans are related to the corals that build reefs. Instead of a hard, stony skeleton, a sea fan has a single, flexible stalk with several side branches. Small polyps located along the feathery branches catch plankton in their tiny tentacles.

Ww
Xx

Whale shark

The whale shark is the world's largest fish and is found throughout the warmer parts of the oceans. Unlike most other sharks, the whale shark does not hunt individual prey. Instead it feeds on plankton, which it filters from the water with its gills.

Max length: 46 feet (14 m)

Xenocongrid eel

Max length: 8 inches (20 cm) This small fish lives around isolated islands in the Indian and Pacific oceans. It is sometimes called the false-moray because it has the same wide jaws and narrow body as the moray eel. But in fact, the xenocongrid eel is completely misnamed because it is not related to eels at all.

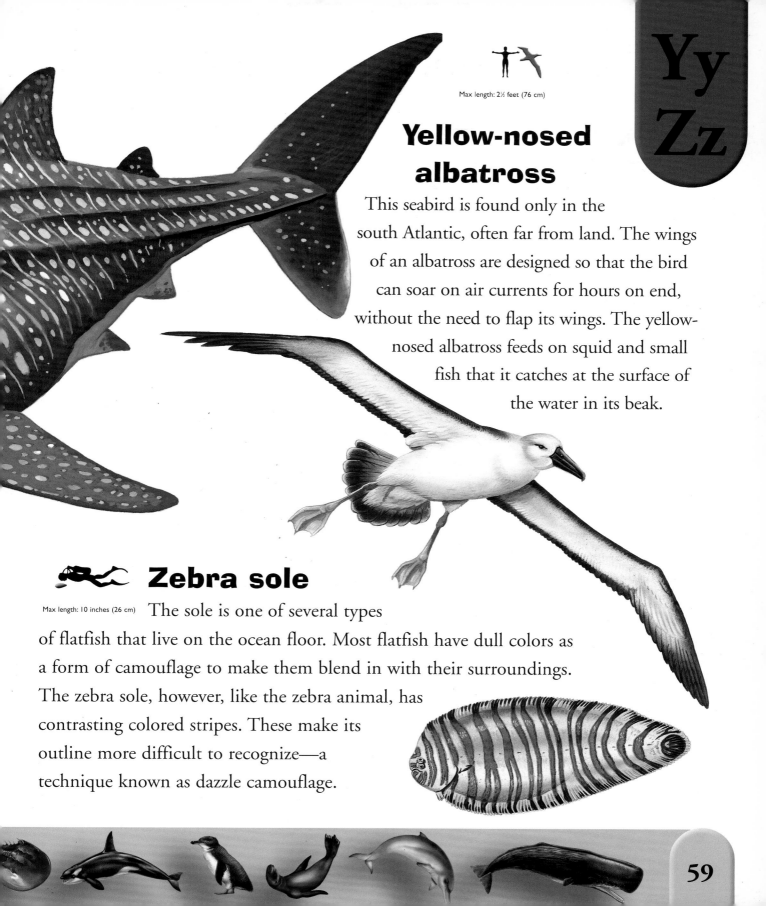

Max length: 2½ feet (76 cm)

Yellow-nosed albatross

This seabird is found only in the south Atlantic, often far from land. The wings of an albatross are designed so that the bird can soar on air currents for hours on end, without the need to flap its wings. The yellow-nosed albatross feeds on squid and small fish that it catches at the surface of the water in its beak.

Zebra sole

Max length: 10 inches (26 cm)

The sole is one of several types of flatfish that live on the ocean floor. Most flatfish have dull colors as a form of camouflage to make them blend in with their surroundings. The zebra sole, however, like the zebra animal, has contrasting colored stripes. These make its outline more difficult to recognize—a technique known as dazzle camouflage.

Glossary

Amphibian An air-breathing animal with a backbone, that lays its eggs in water. Frogs, toads, newts, and salamanders are the most commonly encountered types of amphibian.

Antarctic Relating to the region around the South Pole.

Arctic Relating to the region around the North Pole.

Baleen Plates of bristly mouth-bone used by some whales to filter food from seawater.

Bird A warm-blooded animal that has a body covered with feathers and that lays hard-shelled eggs.

Bird of prey Any bird that hunts and eats other birds, mammals, reptiles, amphibians, or fish.

Bivalve A mollusk, such as the clam, with two shells (scientifically known as valves) that are joined by a hinge.

Continent One of the large landmasses that enclose the seas and oceans.

Crustacean A type of multi-legged animal that is found almost exclusively in the sea. Crabs, shrimp, and lobsters are all crustaceans.

Deep water In the sea, deep water means more than 660 feet (200 m) deep. Some animals live at depths of 6,600 feet (2,000 m) or more.

Dolphin One of a group of toothed whales—the dolphin is a fish-shaped mammal that has become completely adapted to life in water.

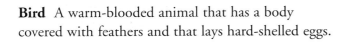

Fin A body part, which projects from the back or sides of a fish. Most fish have at least three fins, one running above the backbone, and one on each side of the body. Most bony fish have fragile fins that are stiffened by rods of hard material. Shark fins are covered with the same tough skin as their bodies. Rays do not have normal fins, but have developed muscular "wings." The projection on the back of a whale or dolphin is known as its fin; those at its side are called flippers (as with seals).

Fish A water-living animal that has a body covered with scales and which breathes through gills.

Freshwater Rainwater, river water, and the water in most lakes is called freshwater because it contains no salt.

Gastropod The scientific name for a snail or slug, both of which are types of mollusk.

Gills The organs that fish, and some other water animals, use to breathe underwater. In most fish, the gills are visible as one or more slits on the sides of the head.

Jaws The hinged bones of the mouth that hold the teeth.

Kelp Seaweed that grows in long strands that are anchored to the seabed. Along some coasts, kelp forms "forests" that attract many sea creatures.

Lagoon A shallow coastal lake formed when sand dunes or a reef cut off a part of the sea.

Mammal A warm-blooded vertebrate animal that produces live-born young. Most mammals are covered with hair and live on land. There are a few marine mammals, such as seals and whales.

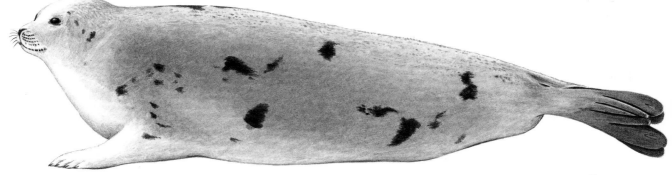

Glossary

Marine Describes anything to do with the seas and oceans.

Migration The regular movement of animals from one place to another. Some birds and whales migrate thousands of miles each year.

Minerals Naturally occurring chemicals, some of which are essential for living things.

Mollusk One of a group of soft-bodied animals. Some mollusks, for example snails, make hard, protective shells for themselves. Another group of mollusks, which includes the octopus and squid, have no external shell, and are equipped with long, grasping tentacles.

Oxygen The chemical gas in air, which is essential for living things. Land animals take in oxygen directly from the air. Fish and most other sea creatures extract oxygen that is dissolved in seawater.

Parasite An animal that lives in or on the body of another animal (called the host) and which feeds on that host.

Ray A type of fish, related to sharks, that has a very flat body. Many rays have a whip-like tail with one or more sharp spines.

Reef An expanse of rock just below the surface of the sea in coastal waters. Coral reefs have a surface layer of living coral animals, and are found only in tropical and subtropical regions.

Reptile A cold-blooded vertebrate that breathes air and produces eggs with leathery shells. Some reptiles give birth to live young. Crocodiles, lizards, turtles, tortoises, and snakes are all reptiles.

Polar Relating to the regions around the North and South poles.

Predator An animal that hunts and eats other animals.

Prey An animal that is hunted and eaten by others.

Glossary

School A large group of fish swimming in the same direction.

Seaweed Non-flowering plants (known as algae) that can grow below the surface of the ocean.

Shallow water In the sea, shallow water ranges from ankle-depth to about 300 feet (100 m) deep.

Shellfish A non-scientific term for sea creatures, such as crustaceans and some mollusks, which have a hard outer shell.

Snout The foremost part of an animal's head, usually the part just above, or around, the mouth.

Species The particular scientific group to which an individual animal (or plant) belongs. Each species has a unique design and two-part scientific name. Members of the same species all share the same characteristics and differ only slightly in coloration or size.

Tentacles The long, boneless limbs of some sea creatures. Tentacles are used for catching prey and are sometimes equipped with stings.

Tropical Belonging to the geographical region around the Equator, between the Tropic of Cancer and the Tropic of Capricorn. The tropical climate is usually hot and rainy.

Venom A poison produced by an animal for the specific purpose of injuring another animal.

Index